New Curricul
MATHEMA
for Schools

Key Stage 1   Book 6

Name _____

Liz and Tony have won 6 coconuts.
They share them equally.
How many coconuts does each child get?

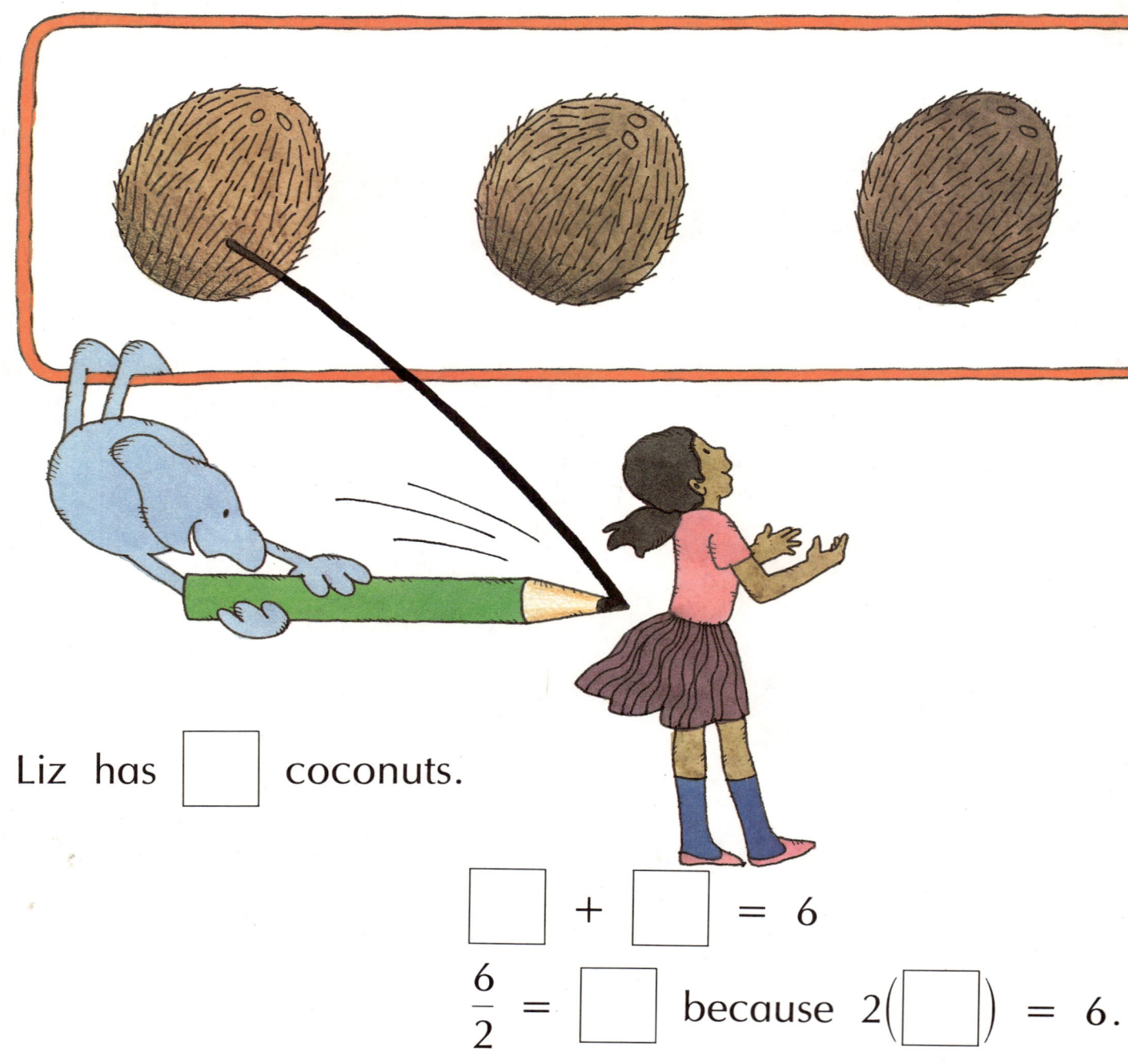

Liz has ☐ coconuts.

☐ + ☐ = 6

$\dfrac{6}{2}$ = ☐ because 2(☐) = 6.

Tony has ☐ coconuts.

A set of 6 makes 2 matching sets. We write $\frac{6}{2}$.

Share 6 cakes equally among 3 children.
How many does each child get?

Each child has ☐ cakes.

☐ + ☐ + ☐ = 6

$\frac{6}{3}$ = ☐ because 3(☐) = 6

A set of 6 makes 3 matching sets. We write $\frac{6}{3}$.

Share 8 sweets equally among 4 children.
How many does each child get?

Each child has ☐ sweets.

☐ + ☐ + ☐ + ☐ = 8

$\frac{8}{4}$ = ☐ because 4(☐) = 8

A set of 8 makes 4 matching sets. We write ....

Share 10 biscuits equally between Susan and Linda.
How many does each girl get?

Each girl has ☐ biscuits. They have **half** each.

$$\frac{10}{2} = \boxed{}$$ because $2\left(\boxed{}\right) = 10$

A set of .... makes .... matching sets. We write $\frac{10}{2}$.

Share 12 biscuits equally between Peter and Paul.
How many does each boy get?

Each boy has ☐ biscuits. They have .... each.

$$\frac{12}{2} = \boxed{}$$ because $2\left(\boxed{}\right) = 12$

A set of .... makes .... matching sets. We write ....

David buys 3 packets of mints.

How much does he spend?

1 packet of mints costs ☐ p.

3 packets of mints cost

☐ p + ☐ p + ☐ p = ☐ p

3(☐ p) = ☐ p

Mike buys 4 packets of chews.

How much does he spend?

1 packet of chews costs ☐ p.

4 packets of chews cost

☐ p + ☐ p + ☐ p + ☐ p = ☐ p

4(☐ p) = ☐ p

Asha buys 4 packets of gums.

How much does she spend?

I packet of gums costs ☐p.

4 packets of gums cost

☐p + ☐p + ☐p + ☐p = ☐p

4(☐p) = ☐p

Ben buys 3 bars of chocolate.

How much does he spend?

I bar of chocolate costs ☐p.

3 bars of chocolate cost

☐p + ☐p + ☐p = ☐p

3(☐p) = ☐p

Jane buys 5 apples.

How much does she spend?

I apple costs ☐p.

5 apples cost

☐p + ☐p + ☐p + ☐p + ☐p = ☐p

5(☐p) = ☐p

Total the bills.

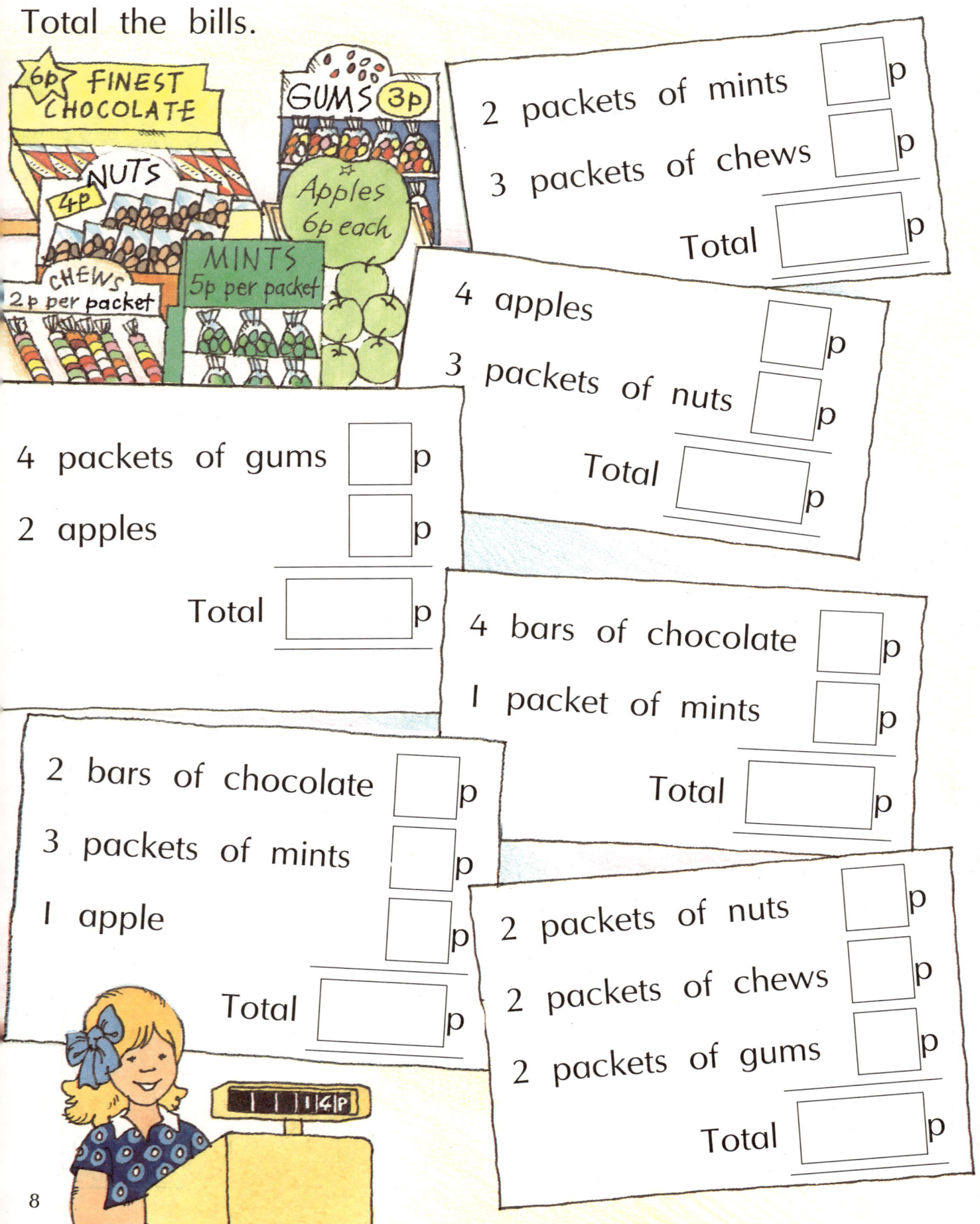

2 packets of mints ☐ p

3 packets of chews ☐ p

Total ☐ p

4 apples ☐ p

3 packets of nuts ☐ p

Total ☐ p

4 packets of gums ☐ p

2 apples ☐ p

Total ☐ p

4 bars of chocolate ☐ p

1 packet of mints ☐ p

Total ☐ p

2 bars of chocolate ☐ p

3 packets of mints ☐ p

1 apple ☐ p

Total ☐ p

2 packets of nuts ☐ p

2 packets of chews ☐ p

2 packets of gums ☐ p

Total ☐ p

8

For sale

	1	2	3	4	5	6	7	8	9	10	11	12	Total
Chews													
Gums													
Chocolate													
Nuts													
Apples													
Mints													

Make a graph of the things sold on pages 6, 7 and 8.

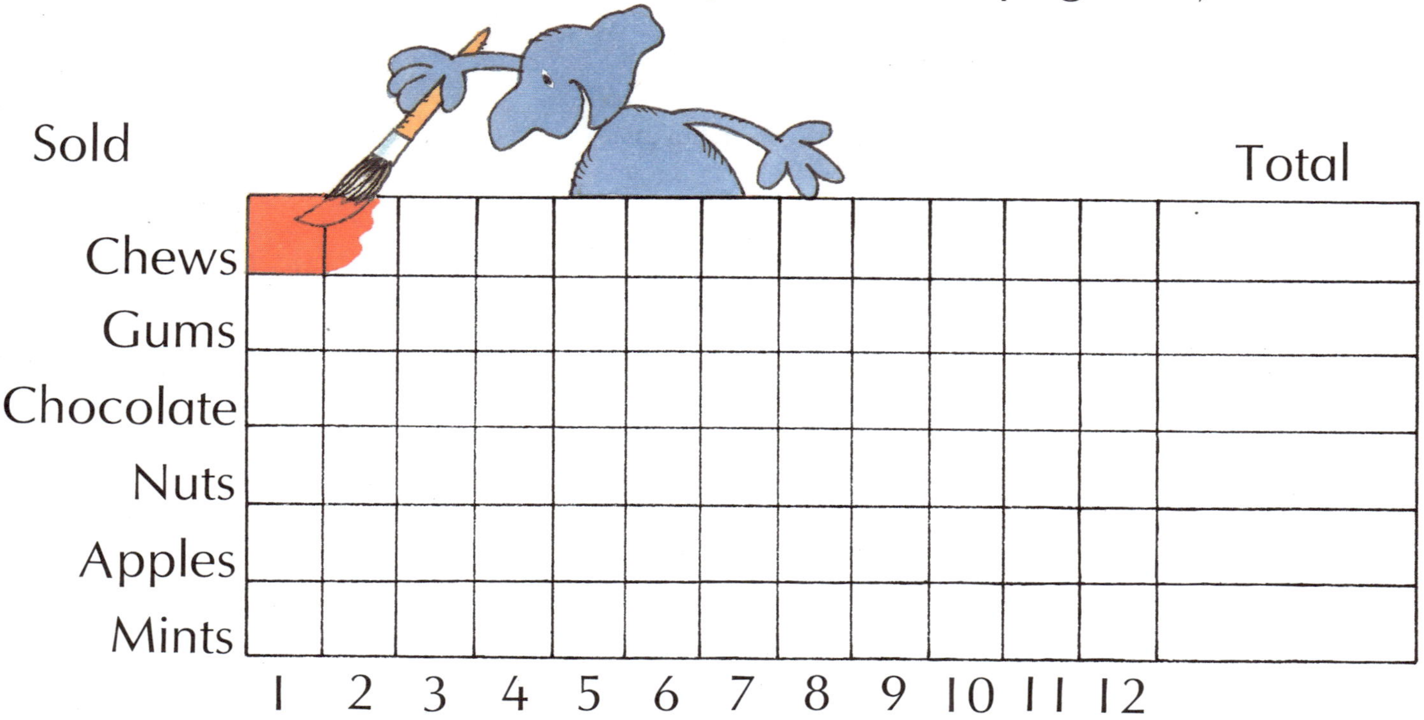

Sold

	1	2	3	4	5	6	7	8	9	10	11	12	Total
Chews													
Gums													
Chocolate													
Nuts													
Apples													
Mints													

Write a 'white paper' about your findings.

There are 8 armbands.

How many children can have 2 armbands each?

Ann   Peter   May   Colin

Ann has ☐ armbands. Peter has ☐ armbands.

May has ☐ armbands. Colin has ☐ armbands.

$$2 + 2 + 2 + 2 = \boxed{}$$

$$4(2) = \boxed{}$$

$$\frac{8}{2} = \boxed{} \text{ because } \boxed{}(2) = 8$$

A set of 8 is made into sets of 2. We write $\frac{8}{2}$.

Put the children into teams.

How many teams?

Put 3 in each team.

$$\frac{9}{3} = \boxed{} \quad \text{because} \quad \boxed{}(3) = 9$$

There are $\boxed{}$ teams.

Put 4 in each team.

$$\frac{8}{4} = \boxed{} \quad \text{because} \quad \boxed{}(4) = 8$$

There are $\boxed{}$ teams.

Put 5 in each team.

$$\frac{10}{5} = \boxed{} \quad \text{because} \quad \boxed{}(5) = 10$$

There are $\boxed{}$ teams.

A set of 10 is made into sets of 5. We write ....

Put 2 flowers in each vase.
How many vases do you need?

$$\frac{10}{2} = \boxed{}$$ because $\boxed{}$ (2) = 10

$\boxed{}$ vases each have 2 flowers.

Put 4 biscuits on each plate.
How many plates do you need?

$$\frac{12}{4} = \boxed{}$$ because $\boxed{}$ (4) = 12

$\boxed{}$ plates each have 4 biscuits.

Put 3 sweets in each box.
How many boxes do you need?

$$\frac{12}{3} = \boxed{}$$ because $\boxed{}$ (3) = 12

$\boxed{}$ boxes each have 3 sweets.

Sophie and Andrew have sorted
their shapes into 4 sets.

They cover the board with shapes
from each set in turn.

Sophie and Andrew find:

☐ of 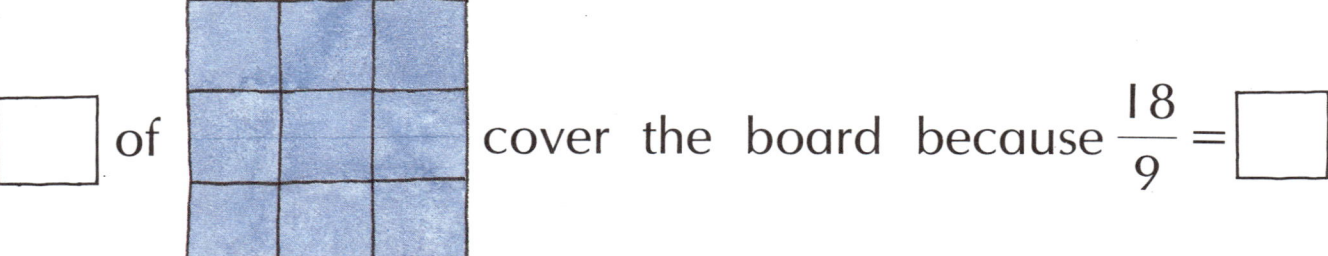 cover the board because $\dfrac{18}{2}=$ ☐

☐ of cover the board because $\dfrac{18}{3}=$ ☐

☐ of cover the board because $\dfrac{18}{6}=$ ☐

☐ of cover the board because $\dfrac{18}{9}=$ ☐

Joe fills the cylinders and the cube with sand from the cartons.

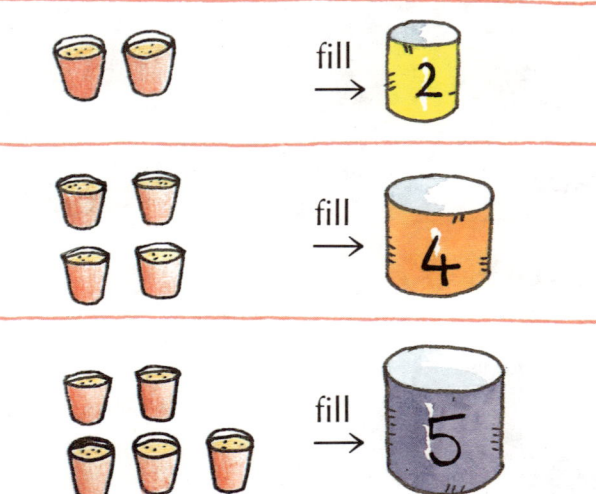

Complete.
Joe finds:

Complete.

$$\frac{20}{2} = \boxed{}$$

$$\frac{20}{5} = \boxed{}$$

$$\frac{20}{4} = \boxed{}$$

Find 3 containers of different sizes.
Estimate how many of your containers
will fill each measure.
Find out if you were correct.

Containers

Half litre measure

	Small	Medium	Large
Estimate			
Result			
Difference			

1 litre measure

	Small	Medium	Large
Estimate			
Result			
Difference			

My plastic box

	Small	Medium	Large
Estimate			
Result			
Difference			

Use unit cubes to build these cuboids.

I used ☐ cubes.

I used ☐ cubes.

I used ☐ cubes.

I used ☐ cubes.

This cuboid is ☐ cubes high.

☐ cubes long.

☐ cubes wide.

I used ☐ cubes.

This cuboid is ☐ cubes high.

☐ cubes long.

☐ cubes wide.

I used ☐ cubes.

How many different cuboids can you make with 36 unit cubes? ☐

Continue the pattern of times. Draw the hands.

8:00

8:05

8:10

Write the times in the boxes.

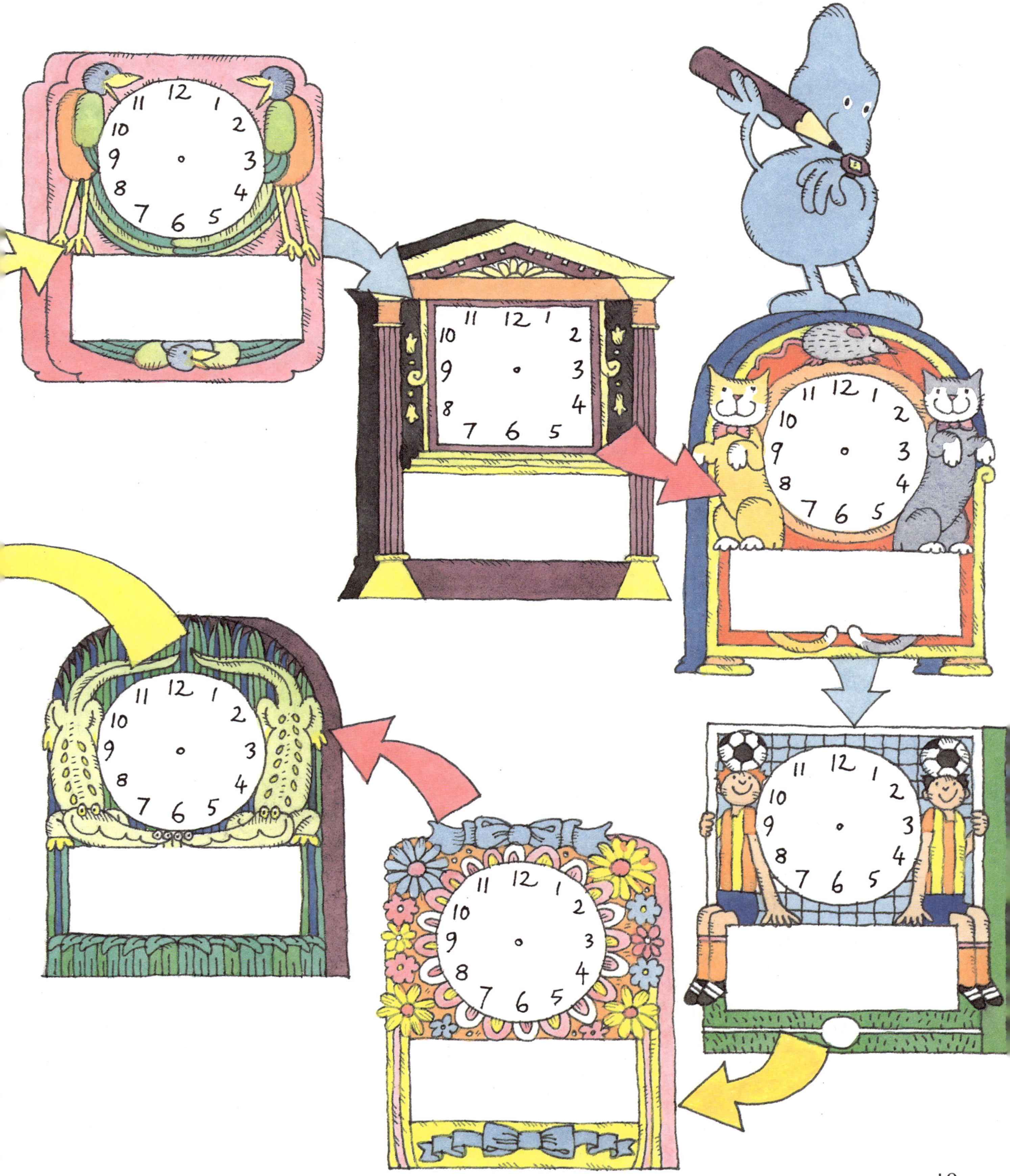

Time travel

The minute hand travels from 12 to 2 in 10 minutes.

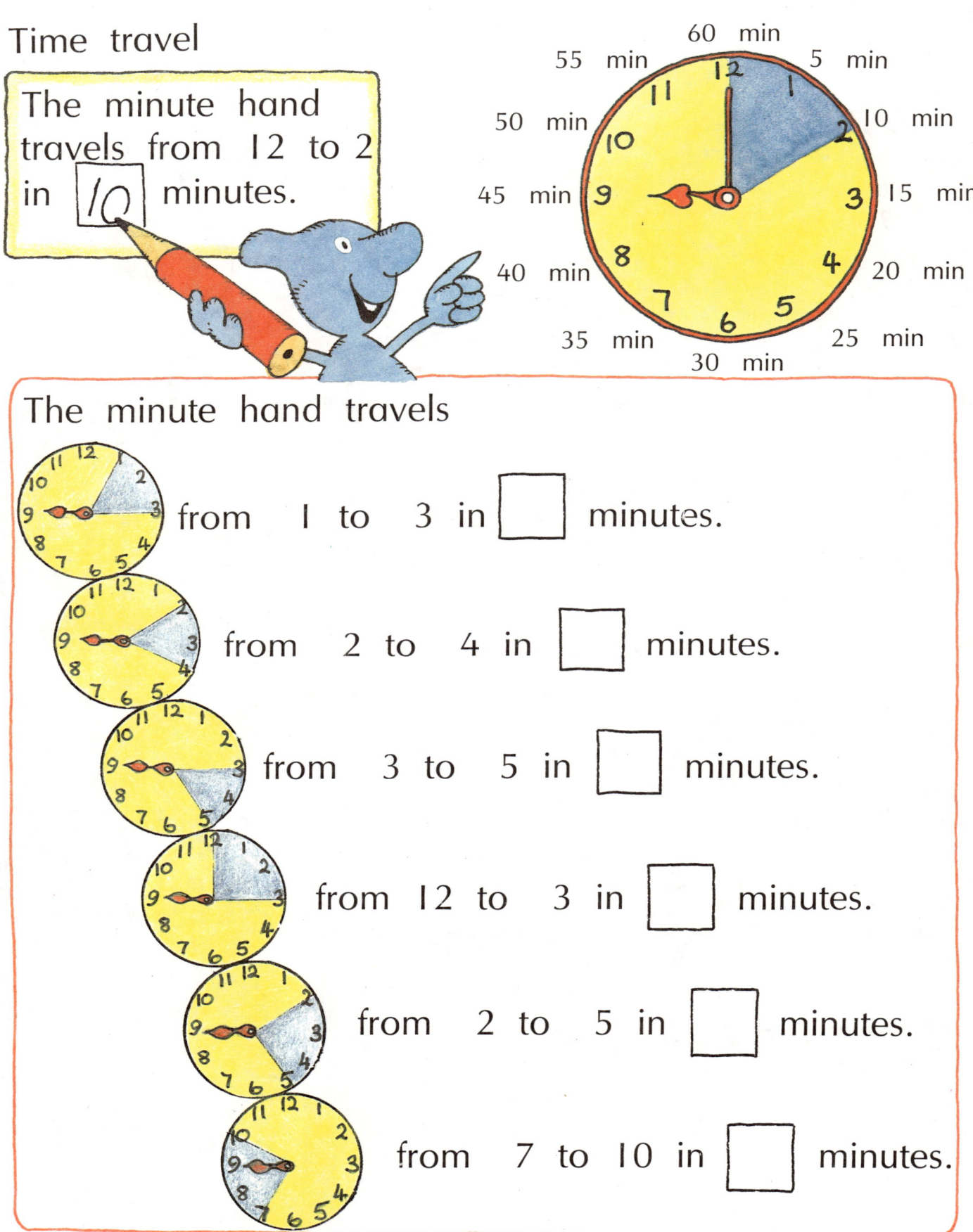

The minute hand travels

from 1 to 3 in ☐ minutes.

from 2 to 4 in ☐ minutes.

from 3 to 5 in ☐ minutes.

from 12 to 3 in ☐ minutes.

from 2 to 5 in ☐ minutes.

from 7 to 10 in ☐ minutes.

Nearly

Just after

It is nearly
6 o'clock.

It is
6 o'clock.

It is just after
6 o'clock.

Complete the sentences.

It is...................

 o'clock.

It is.................

 o'clock.

It is.................

o'clock.

It is...............

 o'clock.

It is.................

 o'clock.

It is.................

 o'clock.

Is it time?

Jim's TV programmes

Playway 2:30	
Sting 4:45	Star-trap 5:15
Cartoons 5 o'clock	Champion 5:40
	News 6 o'clock

Programme	Starts	Time now	Am I in time?
Playway	(clock showing 2:30)	2:45	NO
Sting	(clock)	4:40	
Cartoons	(clock)	4:55	
Star-trap	(clock)	5:30	
Champion	(clock)	5:39	
News	(clock)	6:10	

22

Share equally. Complete the number sentences.

$\frac{12}{2} = $ ☐ because 2 (☐) = 12

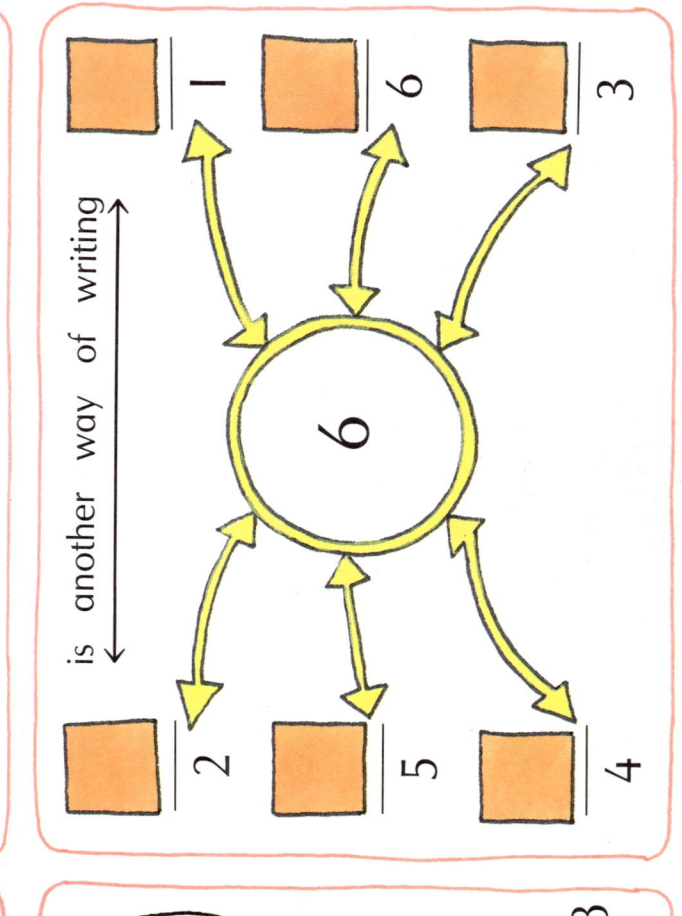

is another way of writing

☐/1 ☐/6 ☐/3

6

☐/2 ☐/5 ☐/4

$\frac{6}{1} = $ ☐ because 1 (☐) = 6

$\frac{18}{3} = $ ☐ because 3 (☐) = 18

23

Draw a picture and write a story for this sentence.

Sally hands out 15 sheets of paper. ☐ children have 5 sheets each.

Complete.

$\dfrac{15}{5}$ = ☐ because ☐ (5) = 15

$\dfrac{20}{4}$ = ☐ because ☐ (4) = 20

$\dfrac{18}{3}$ = ☐ because ☐ (3) = 18

$\dfrac{30}{5}$ = ☐ because 5(☐) = 30

$\dfrac{28}{4}$ = ☐ because ☐ (4) = 28

$\dfrac{5}{5}$ = ☐ because 5(☐) = 5

$\dfrac{12}{4}$ = ☐ because 4(☐) = 12

Pair each story

Tom shares 30 sweets equally among 5 friends. Each friend has ☐ sweets.

$\dfrac{20}{4}$ = ☐ because 4(☐) = 20

$\dfrac{12}{3}$ = ☐ because 3(☐) = 12

$\dfrac{28}{7}$ = ☐ because ☐(7) = 28

$\dfrac{15}{5}$ = ☐ because 5(☐) = 15

$\dfrac{5}{1}$ = ☐ because 1(☐) = 5

$\dfrac{18}{6}$ = ☐ because ☐(6) = 18

$\dfrac{30}{5}$ = ☐ because ☐(5) = 30

with a number sentence.

Draw a picture and write a story for this sentence.

5 friends share 15 toy cars equally. They each have ☐ toy cars.

Zoe has 30 stamps to give away. She gives 5 each to ☐ friends.

25

Colour half of each shape.
Try different ways.

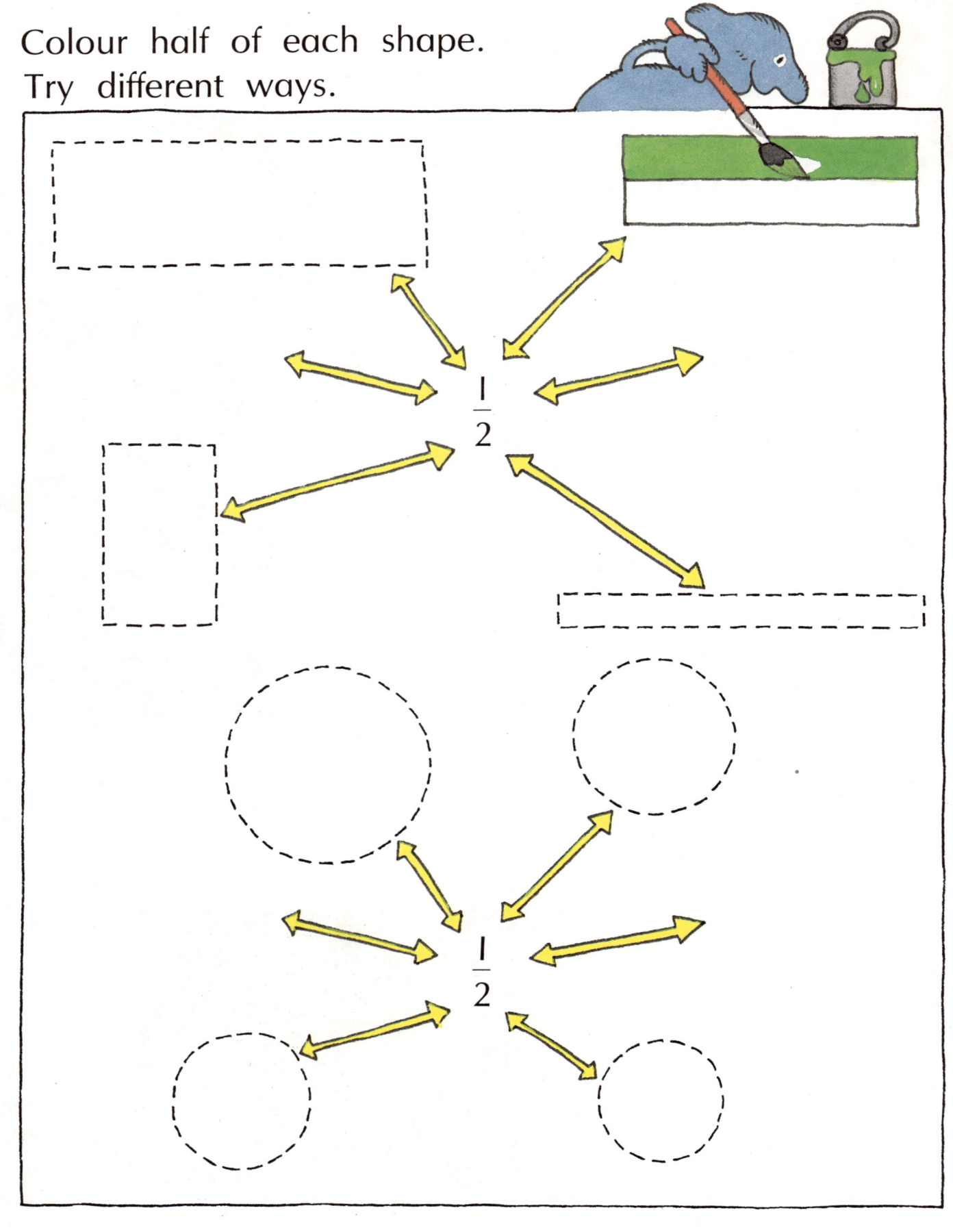

Share 1 bar of fudge equally
between John and Jenny.

John has ☐ and Jenny has ☐ .

☐ + ☐ = 1

$\frac{1}{2}$ + $\frac{1}{2}$ = ☐

Share an apple equally between
Christine and Christopher.

Christine has ☐ and Christopher has ☐ .

☐ + ☐ = 1

$\frac{1}{2}$ + $\frac{1}{2}$ = ☐

Make 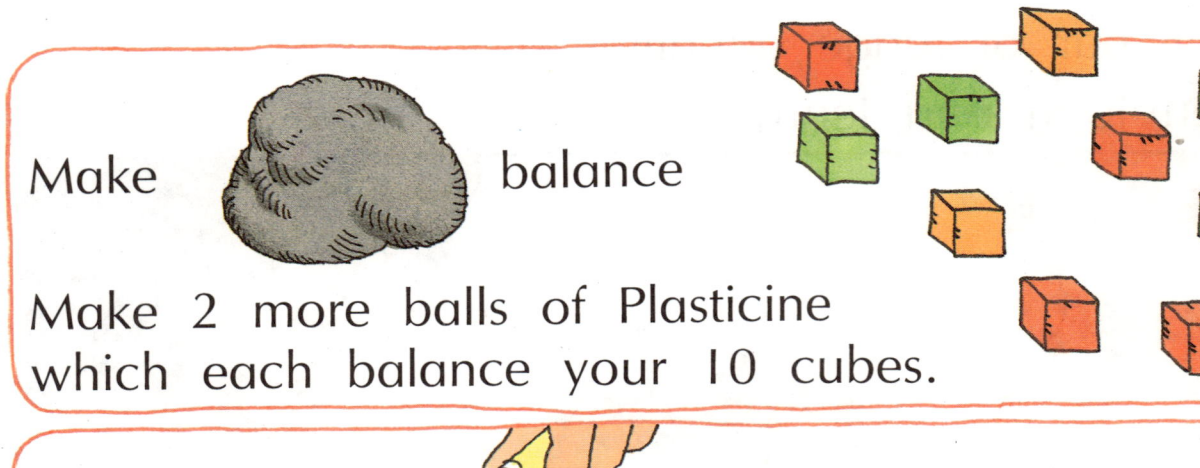 balance

Make 2 more balls of Plasticine which each balance your 10 cubes.

Now cut one ball into 2  so that the pieces balance.

Balance a half ball of Plasticine with some cubes.

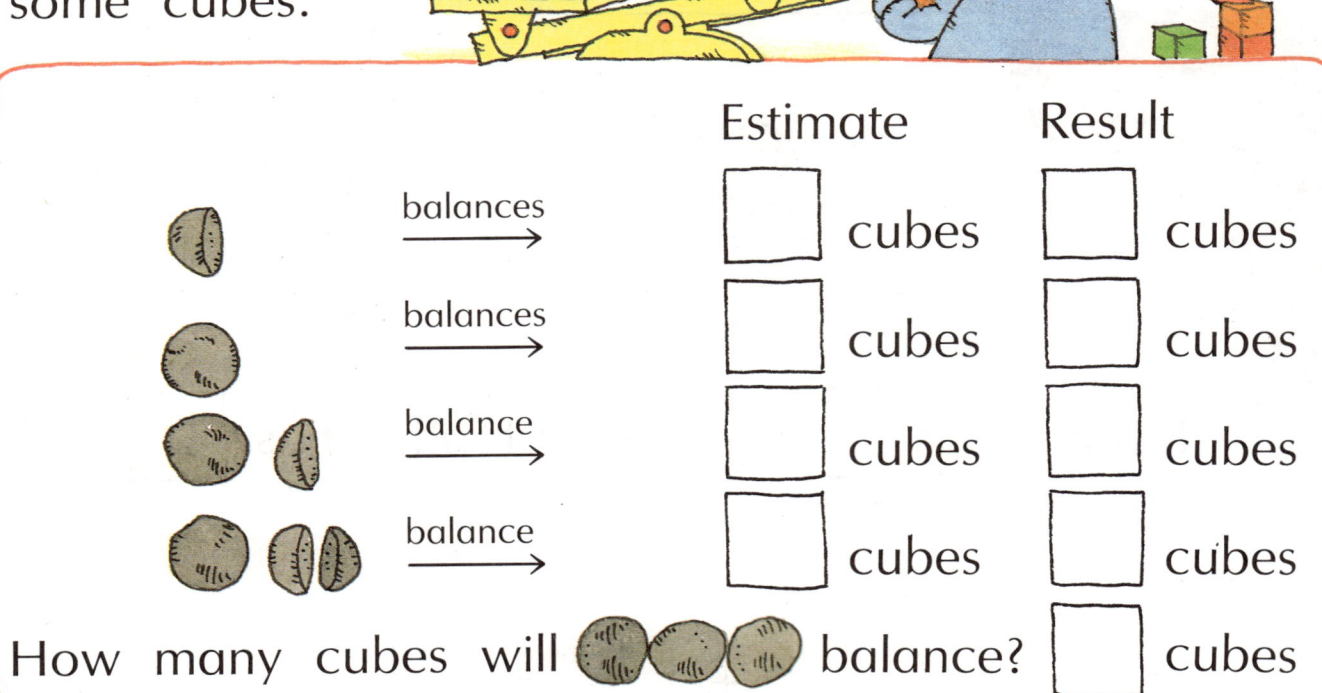

		Estimate	Result
	balances →	☐ cubes	☐ cubes
	balances →	☐ cubes	☐ cubes
	balance →	☐ cubes	☐ cubes
	balance →	☐ cubes	☐ cubes

How many cubes will balance? ☐ cubes

Emma marks the cubes which balance with the counters.
She finds:

2 → balances → (green) (red)

4 → balances → (orange) (grey) (orange) (green)

8 → balances → (orange) (green) (grey) (red) (green) (orange) (red) (grey)

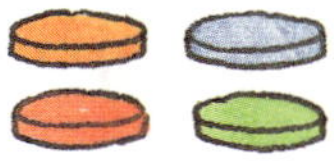

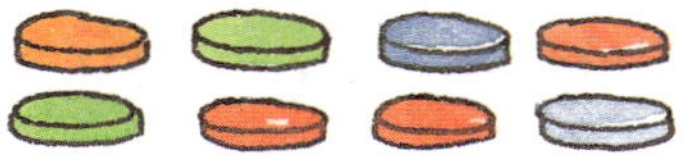

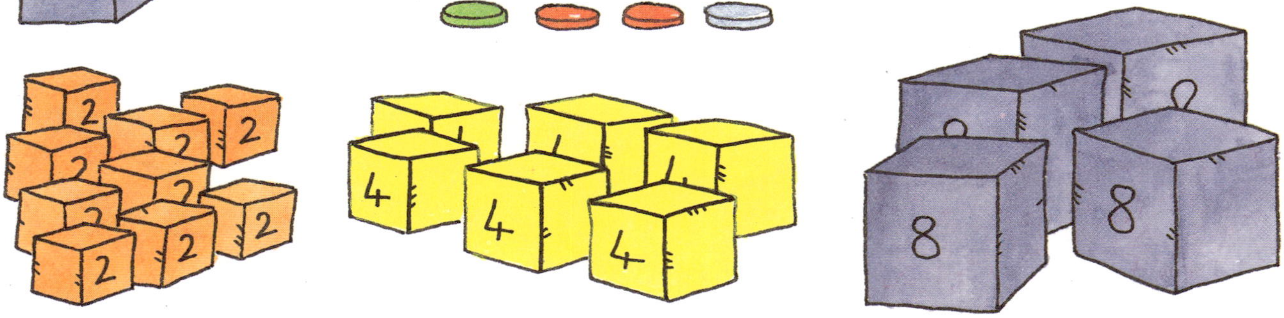

Emma balances 16 counters with cubes from each set.

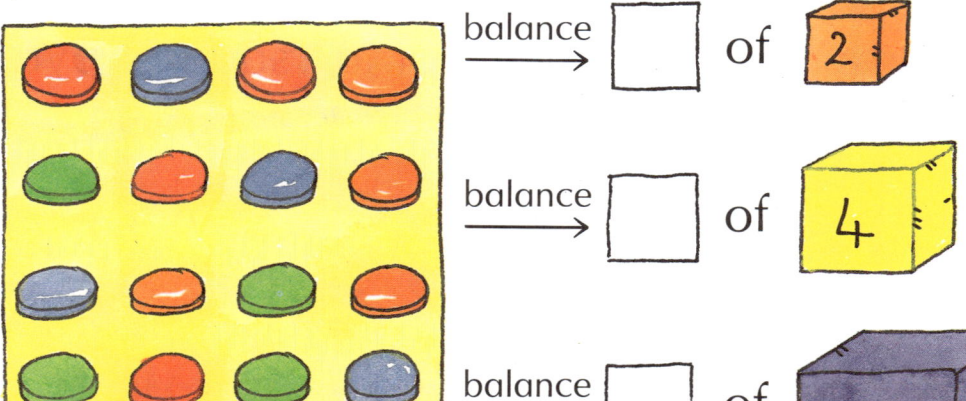

balance → ☐ of 2

balance → ☐ of 4

balance → ☐ of 8

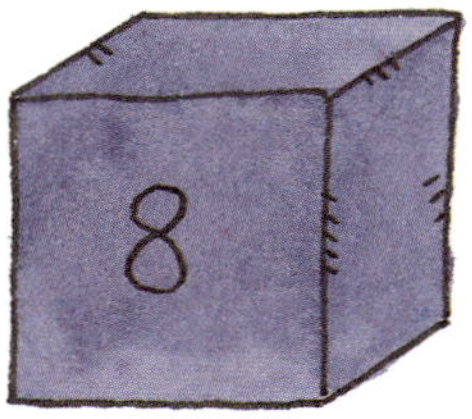

Complete.

$\dfrac{16}{2} = \boxed{}$ $\dfrac{16}{8} = \boxed{}$ $\dfrac{16}{4} = \boxed{}$

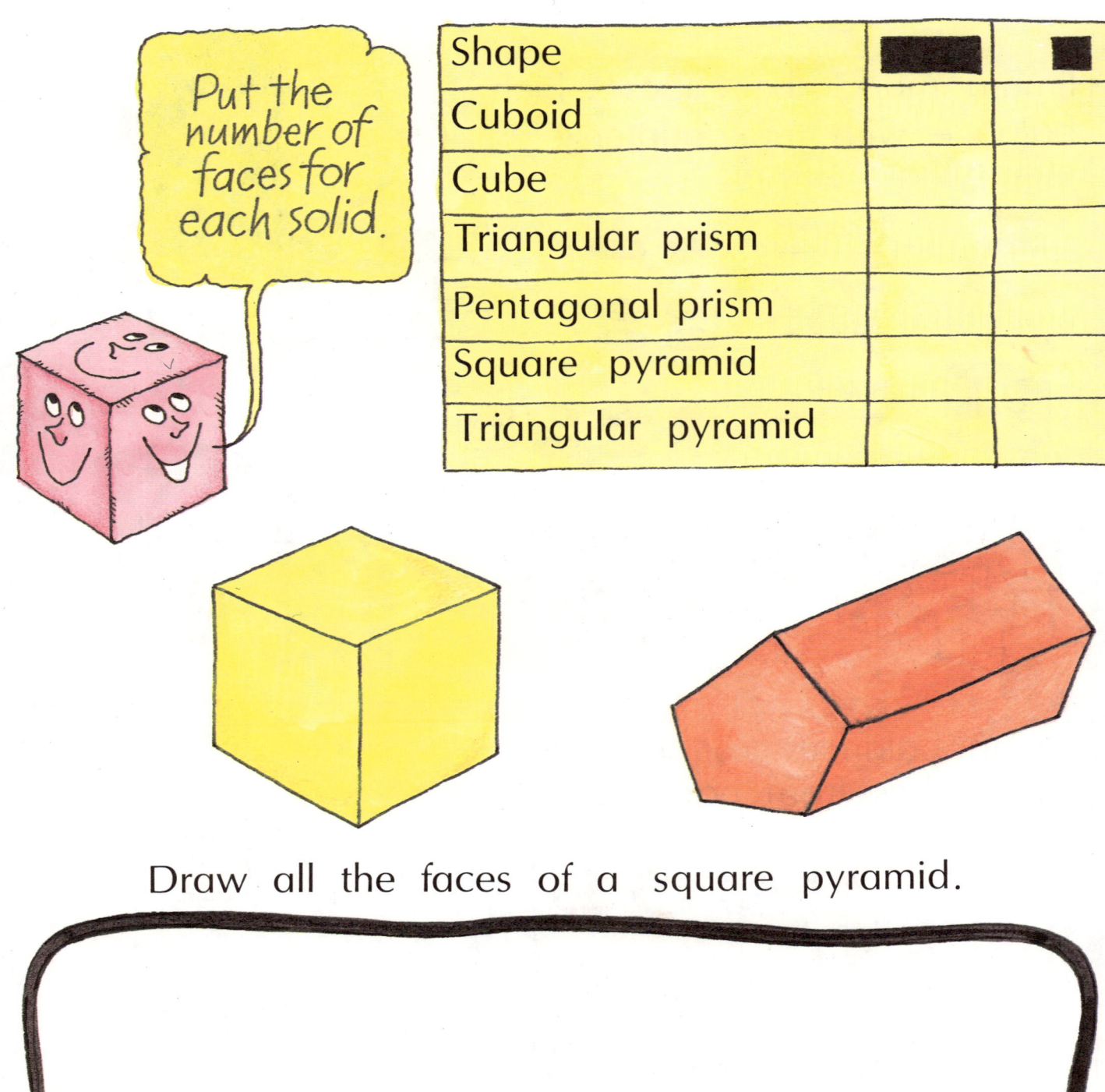

Put the number of faces for each solid.

Shape	▬	■
Cuboid		
Cube		
Triangular prism		
Pentagonal prism		
Square pyramid		
Triangular pyramid		

Draw all the faces of a square pyramid.

▲	⬟	Total faces

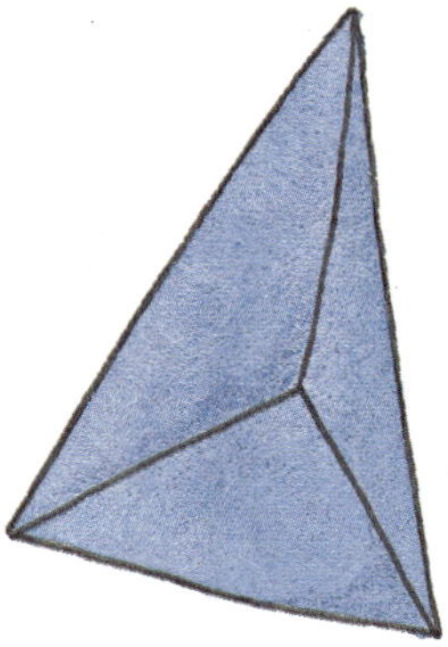

Draw all the faces of a pentagonal prism.

David has 8 triangular tiles
to cover his shape exactly.
Colour the other shapes he can
cover exactly, using all his tiles.

David's shape

Rhian has placed a tile
in each shape.
Complete the tiling for
each shape.

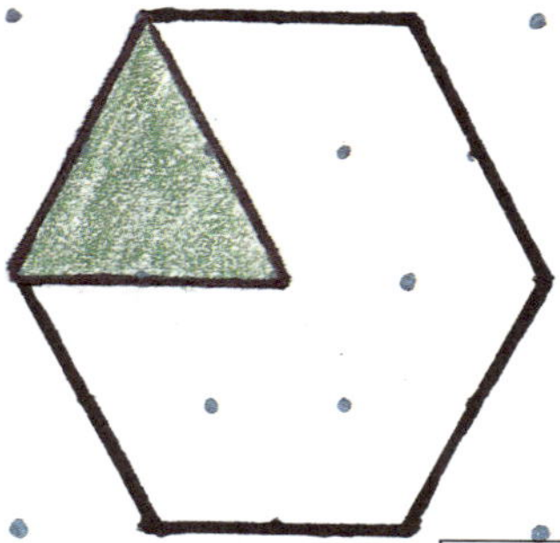

☐ tiles

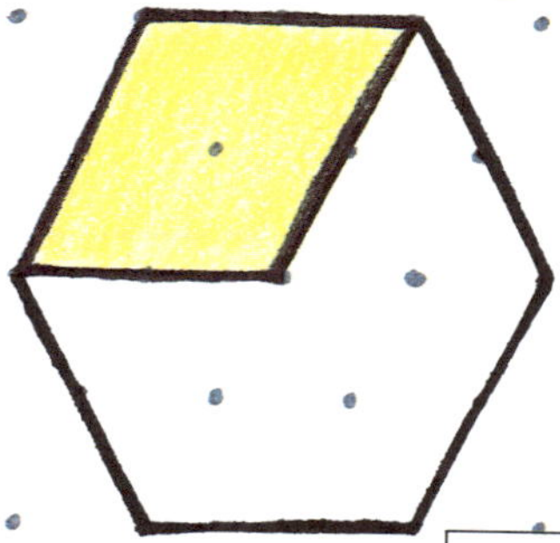

☐ tiles

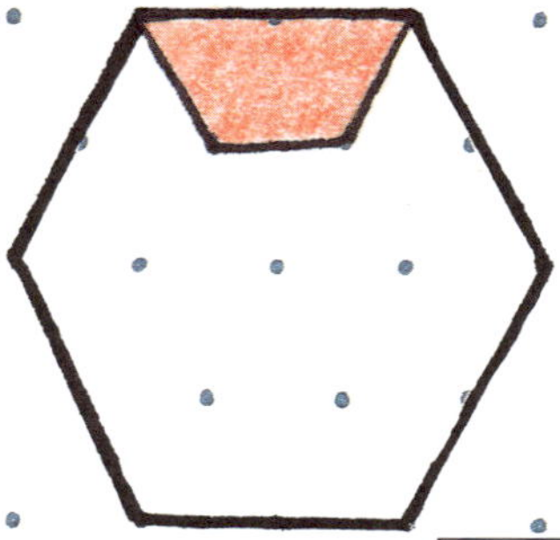

☐ tiles

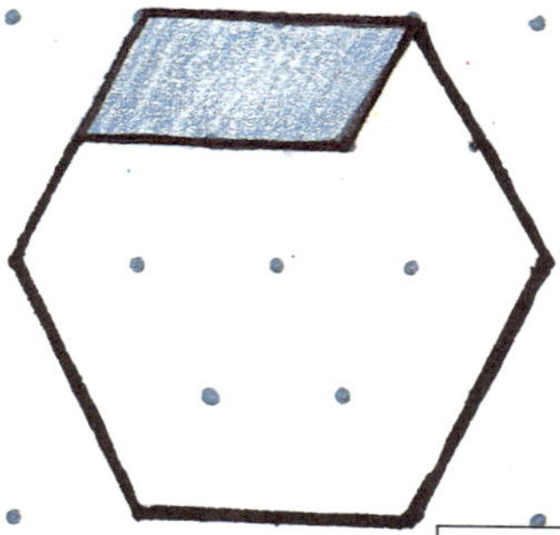

☐ tiles

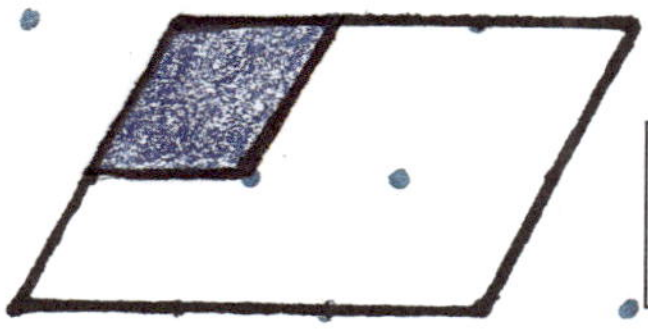

☐ tiles

☐ tiles

☐ tiles

Count the small squares in each shape.
Write your answer in the shape.
Draw some larger squares.

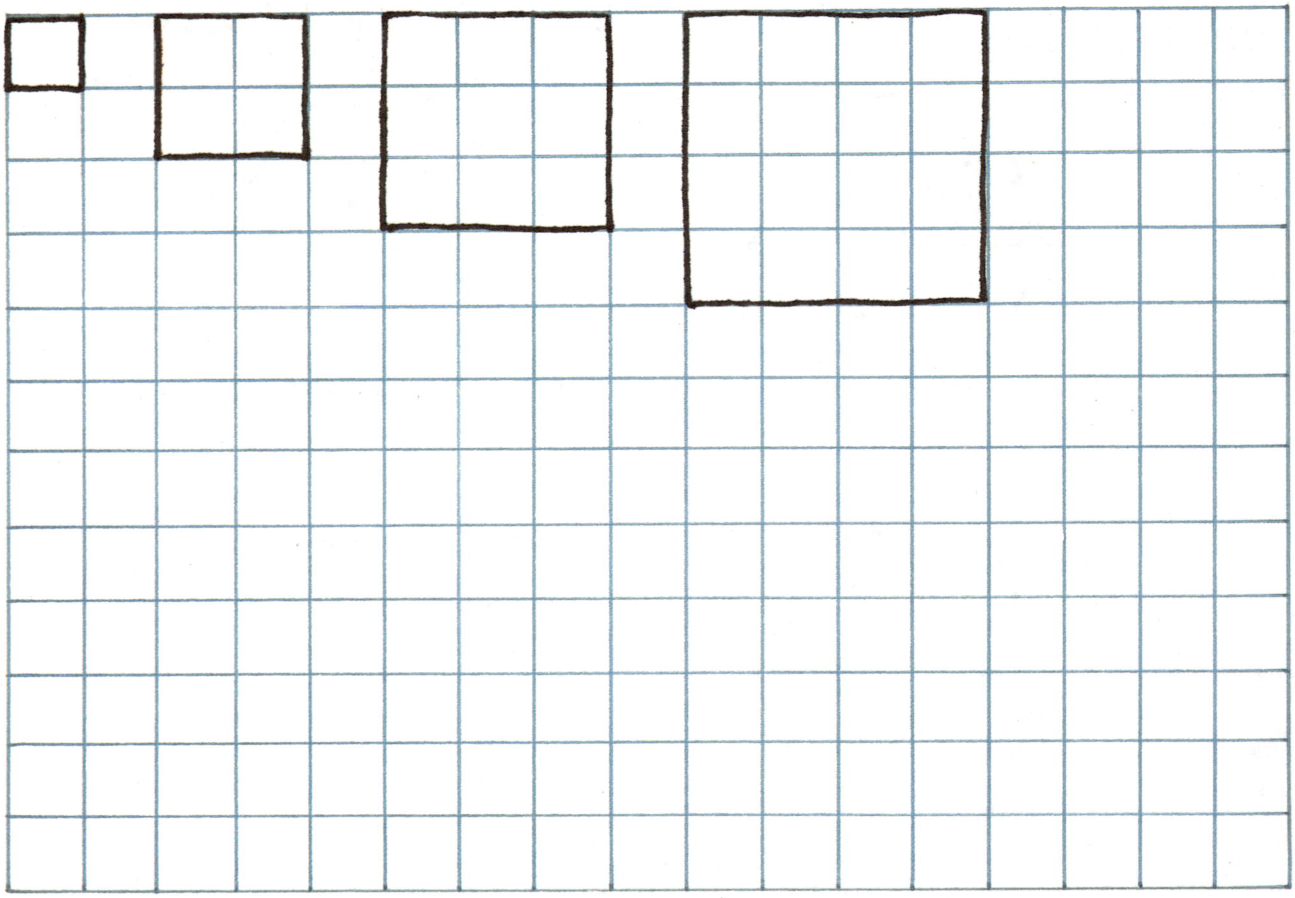

Count the small triangles in each shape.
Write your answer in the shape.
Draw a larger triangle.

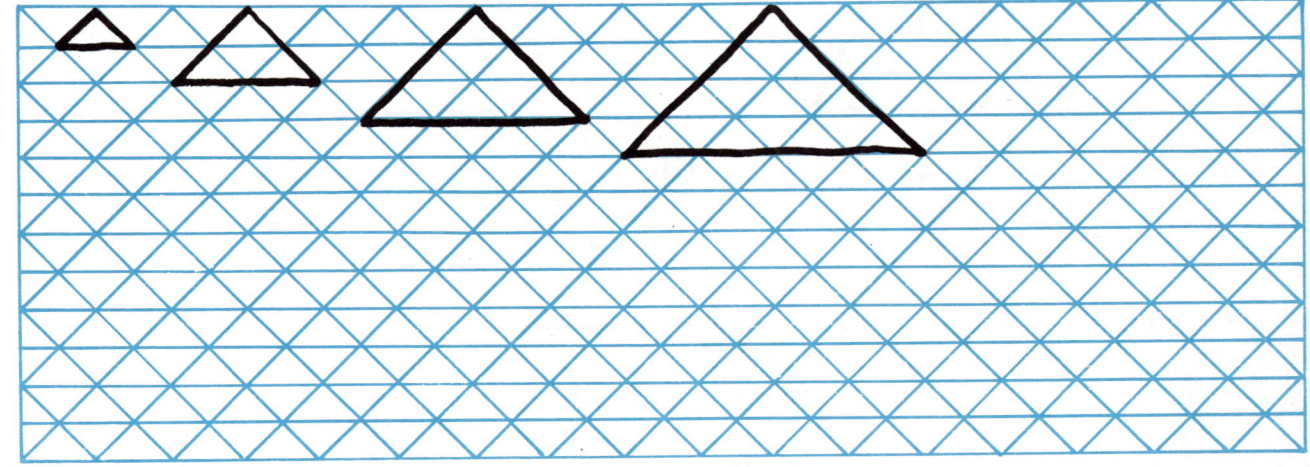

Kirsten sorts 6 stamps in 2 different ways.

First she makes 2 sets of 3.

She has a set of
3 stamps 2 times.

$$2(3) \xrightarrow{\text{can be written}} 3 \times 2$$

$$3 \times 2 = 6$$

Kirsten says:
3 **multiplied by** 2
equals 6.

Then she makes 3 sets of 2.
Complete.

She now has a set of

2 stamps ☐ times.

$$3(\boxed{}) \xrightarrow{} \boxed{} \times 3$$

$$\boxed{} \times 3 = 6$$

Kirsten now says:

....

equals 6.

Ring 3(4).

3(4) = ☐ × 3 = ☐

Ring 4(3).

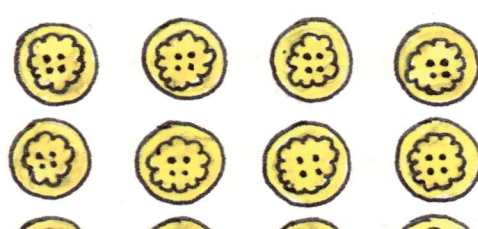

4(3) = ☐ × 4 = ☐

Ring 2(5).

2(5) = ☐ × 2 = ☐

Ring 5(2).

5(2) = ☐ × 5 = ☐

Ring a set of 2 buttons 4 times.

☐ × 4 = ☐

Complete the triples.

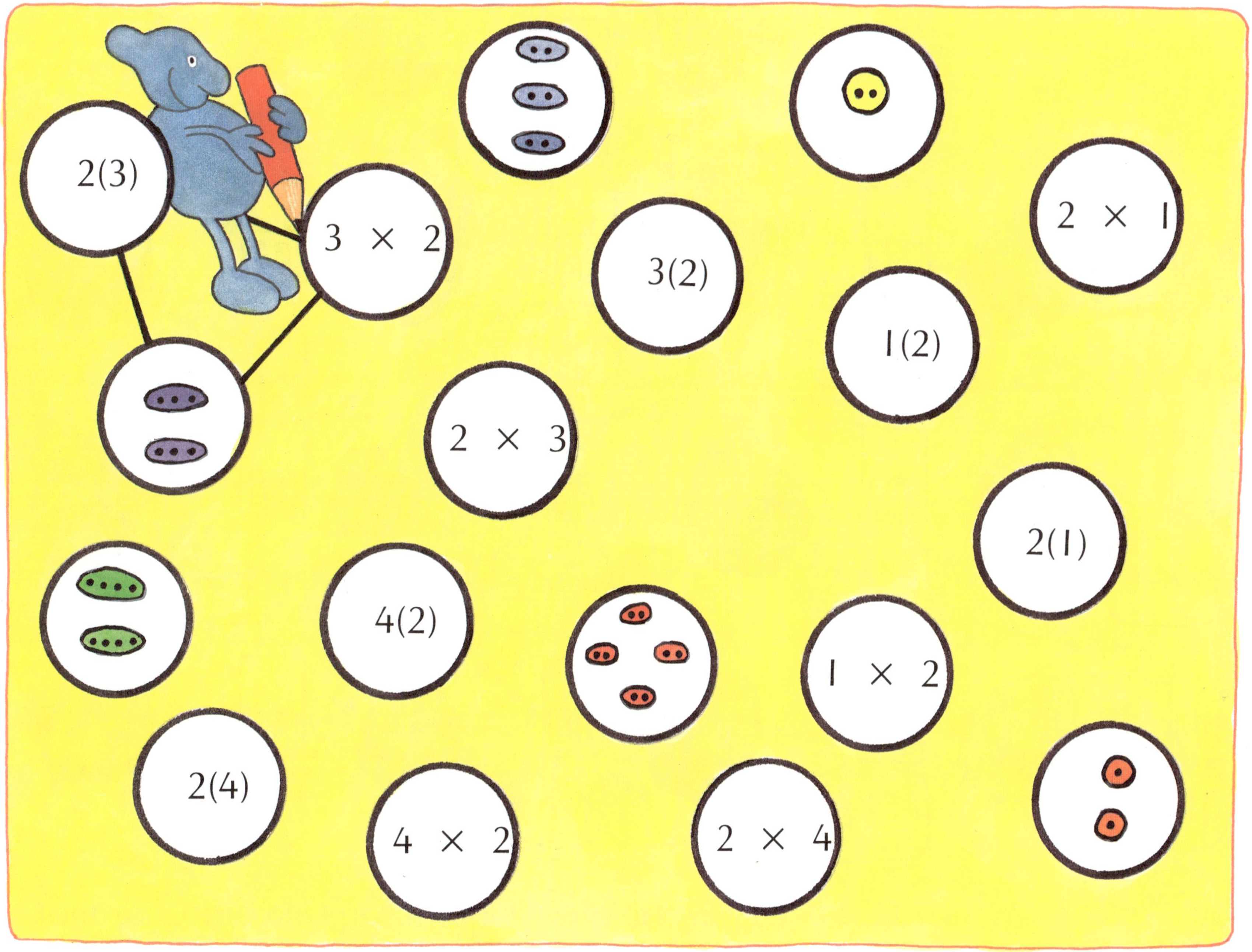

2 × 1

2 (1)

1 (2)

1 × 2

3 (2)

2 × 4

3 × 2

2 × 3

4 (2)

4 × 2

2 (3)

2 (4)

Join to complete the number sentences.

4 × 10   18

7 × 2   15

3 × 3   24

10 × 3   25

5 × 3   40

6 × 3   14

6 × 4   9

4 × 4   10

2 × 4   12

5 × 5   30

5 × 4   6

5 × 2   8

4 × 3   16

3 × 2   20

Sara wants to share 8 plums equally with her friends.

Left panel

If she shares them with Jyoti, she thinks:

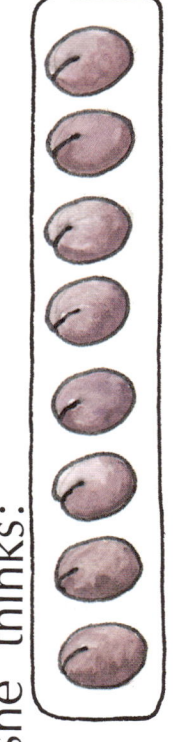

Each will get half the plums.

They will have ☐ each.

$\dfrac{8}{2}$ = ☐ because ☐ × 2 = 8.

$\dfrac{8}{2}$ = ☐ $\xrightarrow[\text{written}]{\text{can be}}$ 8 ÷ 2 = ☐.

Sara says:
8 **divided by** 2 equals ☐.

Right panel

If she shares them with Ann, Ron and John, she thinks:

Each will get a quarter.

They will have ☐ each.

$\dfrac{8}{4}$ = ☐ because ☐ × 4 = 8.

$\dfrac{8}{4}$ = ☐ $\xrightarrow[\text{written}]{\text{can be}}$ 8 .... 4 = ☐.

8 .... 4 equals ☐.

Complete this number sentence: 12 ÷ 4 = ☐. Write a story for it.

Sara is asked to put the apples into bags.

If she puts 5 in a bag, she thinks:

She will need ☐ bags.

$\dfrac{10}{5}$ = ☐ because 5 × ☐ = 10

$\dfrac{10}{5}$ = ☐ $\xrightarrow[\text{written}]{\text{can be}}$ 10 ÷ 5 = ☐

Sara says:

10 divided by 5 equals ☐.

If she puts 2 in a bag, she thinks:

She will need ☐ bags.

$\dfrac{10}{2}$ = ☐ because 2 × ☐ = 10

$\dfrac{10}{2}$ = ☐ $\xrightarrow[\text{written}]{\text{can be}}$ 10 .... 2 = ☐

Sara says:

10 .... 2 equals ☐.

Complete this number sentence: 8 ÷ 2 = ☐. Write a story.

Complete the calculator dominoes.

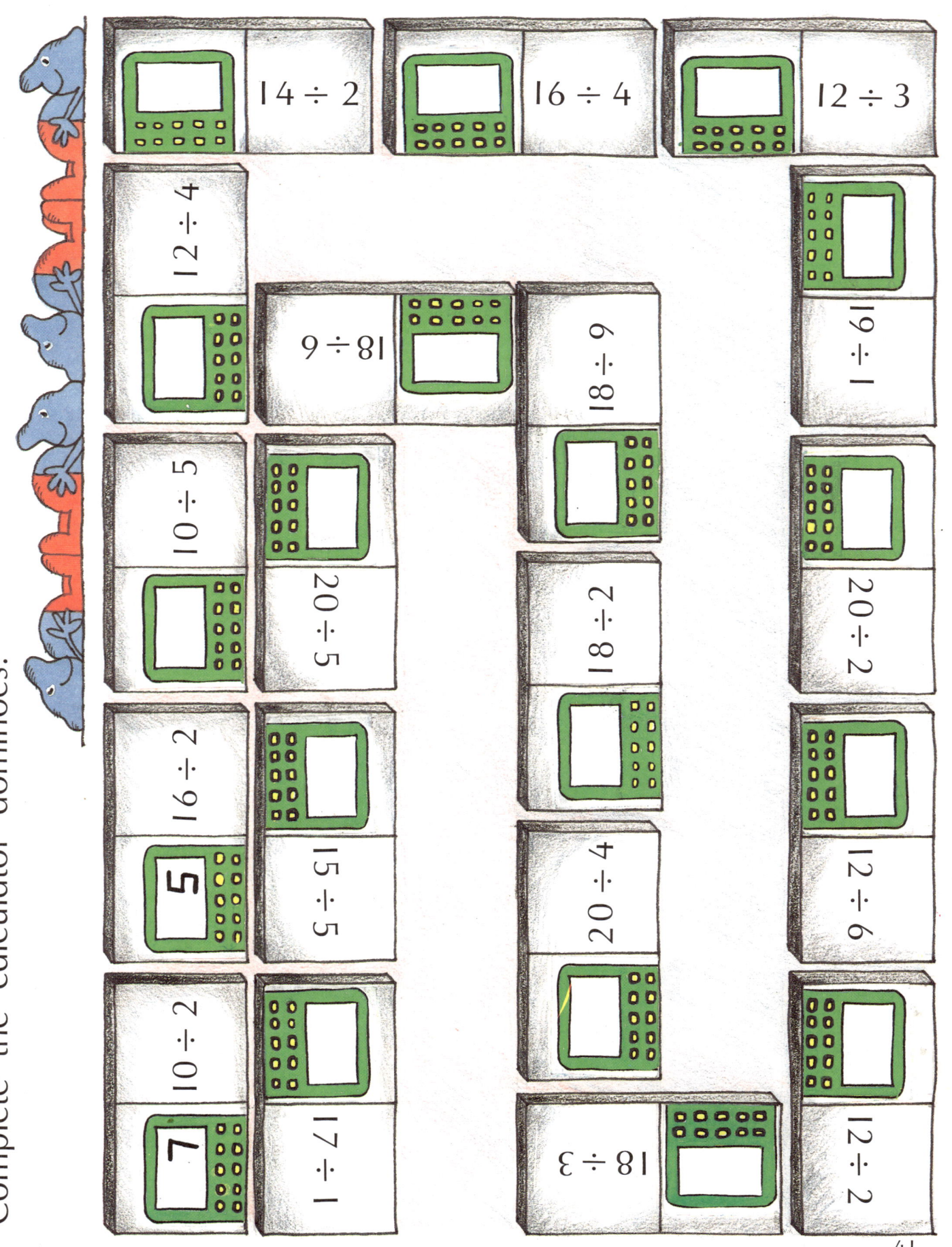

$14 \div 2$

$16 \div 4$

$12 \div 3$

$12 \div 4$

$18 \div 9$

$18 \div 6$

$19 \div 1$

$10 \div 5$

$20 \div 5$

$18 \div 2$

$20 \div 2$

$16 \div 2$

$15 \div 5$

$20 \div 4$

$12 \div 6$

$10 \div 2$

$17 \div 1$

$18 \div 3$

$12 \div 2$

5

7

Continue the pattern of right angle turns.

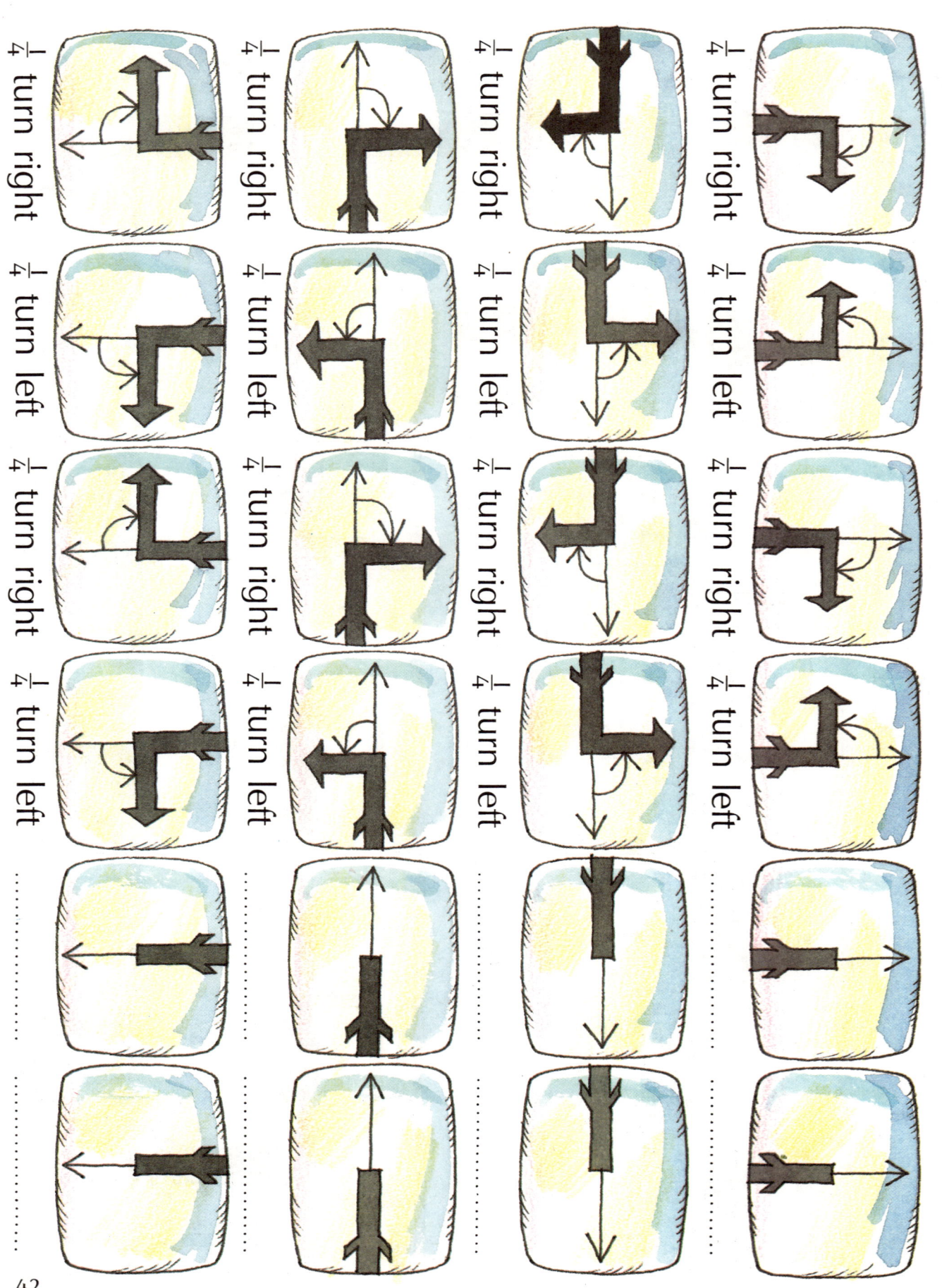

$\frac{1}{4}$ turn right

$\frac{1}{4}$ turn left

$\frac{1}{4}$ turn right

$\frac{1}{4}$ turn left

$\frac{1}{4}$ turn right

$\frac{1}{4}$ turn left

$\frac{1}{4}$ turn right

$\frac{1}{4}$ turn left

$\frac{1}{4}$ turn right

$\frac{1}{4}$ turn right

$\frac{1}{4}$ turn left

$\frac{1}{4}$ turn left

$\frac{1}{4}$ turn right

$\frac{1}{4}$ turn right

$\frac{1}{4}$ turn left

$\frac{1}{4}$ turn left

Start from home each time.
Find where each path ends.

Shop

Playground

Garage

Bridge

Home

1	2	3
Forward 1 street, $\frac{1}{4}$ turn right, forward 1 street, $\frac{1}{4}$ turn left, forward 4 streets. I am at the	Forward 2 streets, $\frac{1}{4}$ turn right, forward 3 streets, $\frac{1}{4}$ turn left, forward 1 street, $\frac{1}{4}$ turn right, forward 2 streets. I am at the	Forward 4 streets, $\frac{1}{4}$ turn right, forward 3 streets, $\frac{1}{4}$ turn right, forward 3 streets, $\frac{1}{4}$ turn left, forward 2 streets. I am at the ....

Find the function.

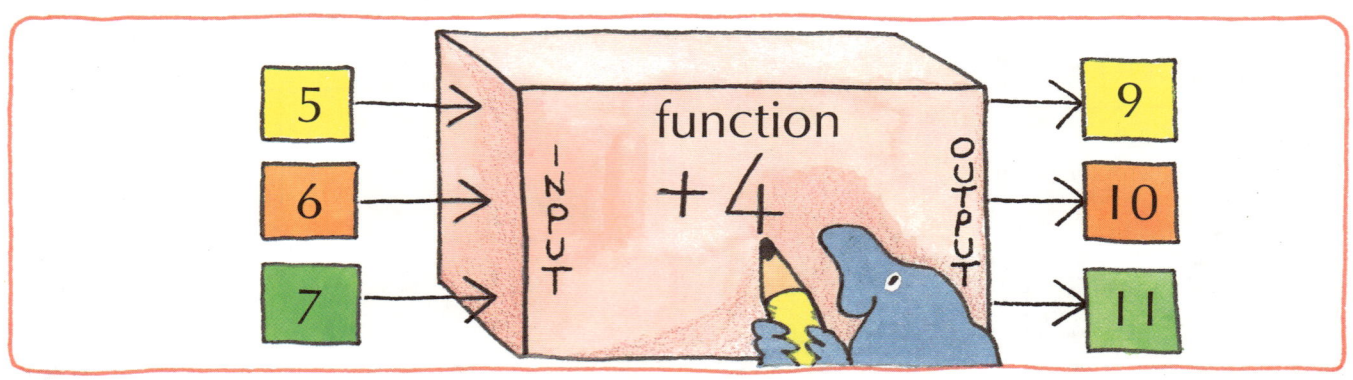

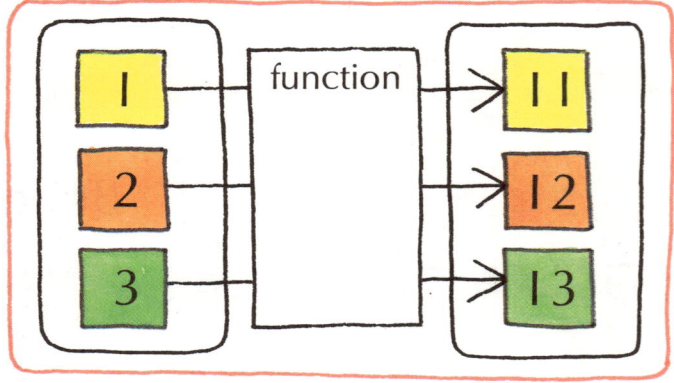

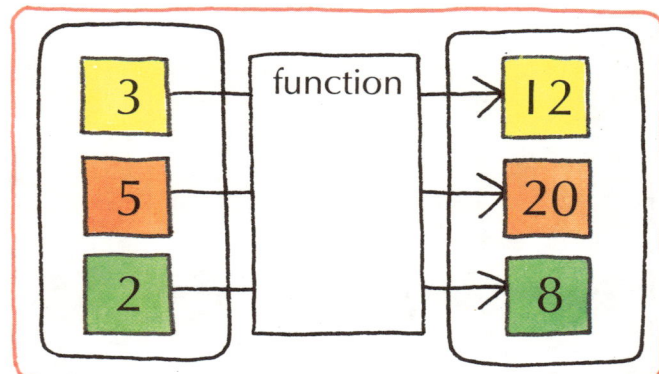

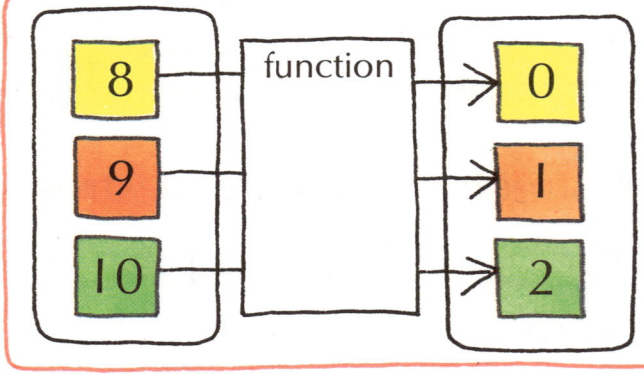

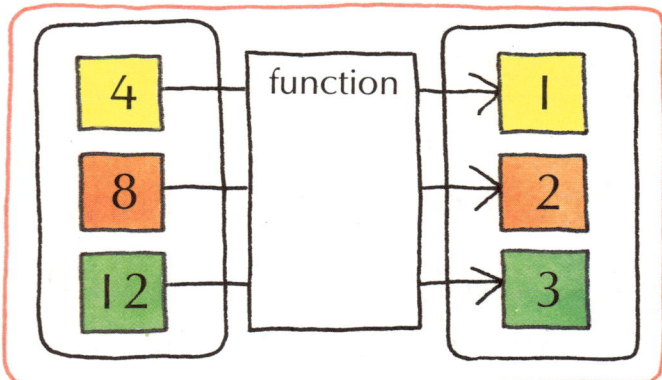

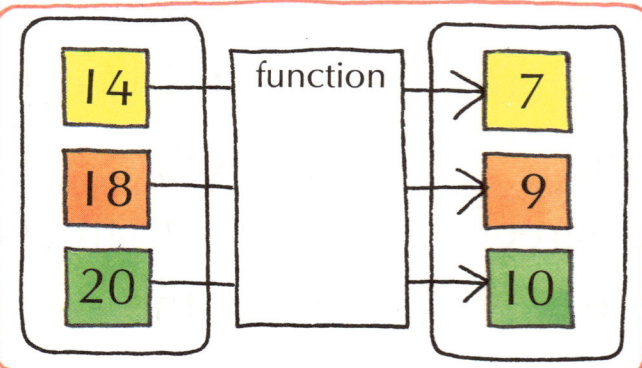

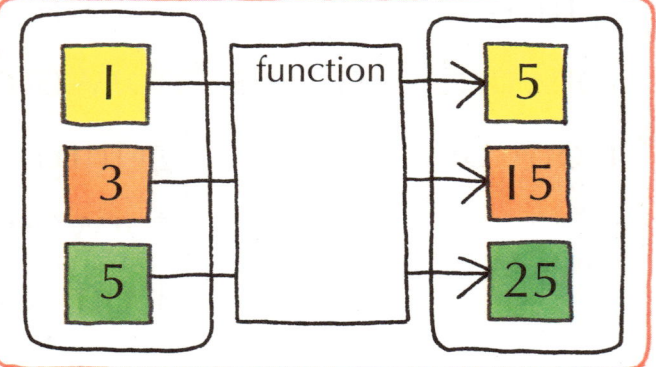

The 2-stage machine

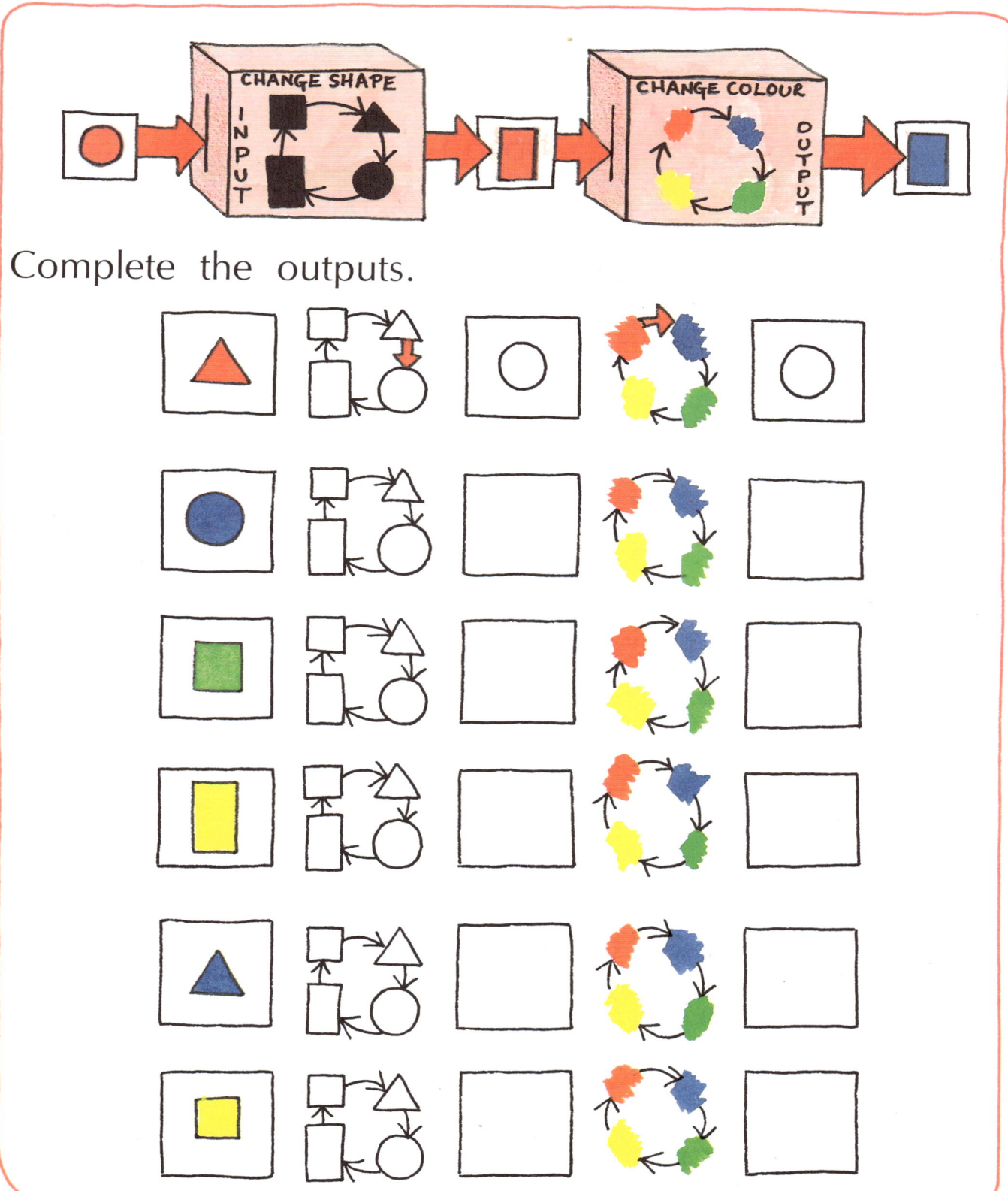

Complete the outputs.

Match.

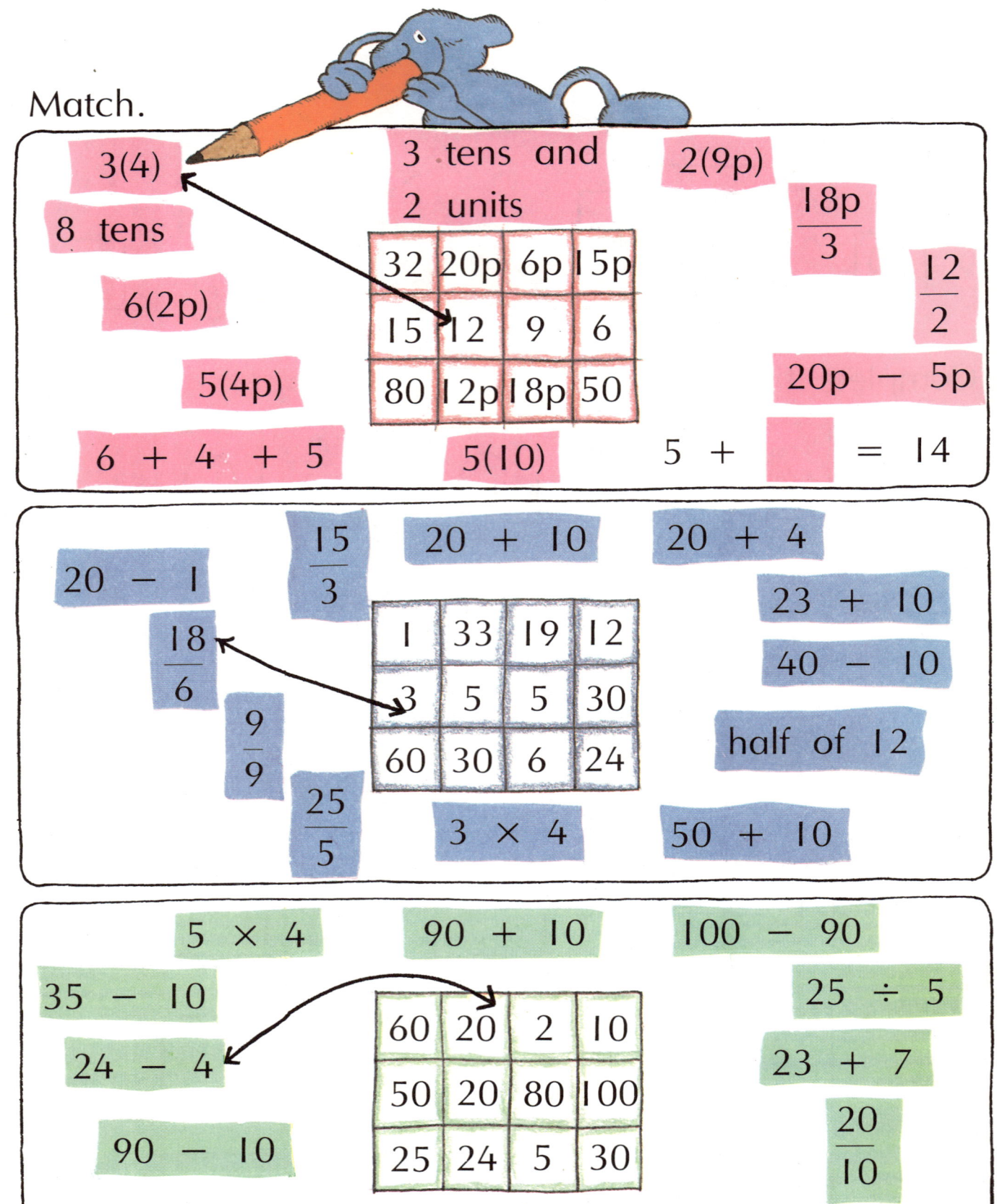

3(4)

8 tens

6(2p)

5(4p)

6 + 4 + 5

3 tens and 2 units

32	20p	6p	15p
15	12	9	6
80	12p	18p	50

5(10)

2(9p)

$\dfrac{18p}{3}$

$\dfrac{12}{2}$

20p − 5p

5 + ☐ = 14

---

20 − 1

$\dfrac{18}{6}$

$\dfrac{9}{9}$

$\dfrac{15}{3}$

20 + 10

20 + 4

23 + 10

40 − 10

half of 12

$\dfrac{25}{5}$

1	33	19	12
3	5	5	30
60	30	6	24

3 × 4

50 + 10

---

5 × 4

90 + 10

100 − 90

35 − 10

24 − 4

90 − 10

60	20	2	10
50	20	80	100
25	24	5	30

25 ÷ 5

23 + 7

$\dfrac{20}{10}$

4 × 6

30 + 20

30 + 30

Pippa has 12p.
Kim has 7p.
Together they have ☐ p.

June has 20 marbles.
She loses 13.
She has ☐ marbles left.

Jamie has 16 sweets. Phil has 9 sweets. Jamie has ☐ more sweets than Phil.

Mum shares 15p equally among Tom, Lucy and Sam. Each has ☐ p.

I have 30p.
I spend 20p on chocolate.
I have ☐ p left.

Raisins cost 3p a packet. I buy 4 packets. I spend ☐ p.

Susie cuts 6 cm from a piece of ribbon 20 cm long.
There are ☐ cm left.

Dad has 15p.
He gives 5p to each child.
There are ☐ children.

New Curriculum
MATHEMATICS
for Schools

Consultant Editor: Sir Wilfred Cockcroft

Illustrated by John Lobban

Authors: John Marshall (*Coordinator*), John Armstrong, John Page, Linda Parton and Gwyn Price.

Solid shapes in Books 1 to 6

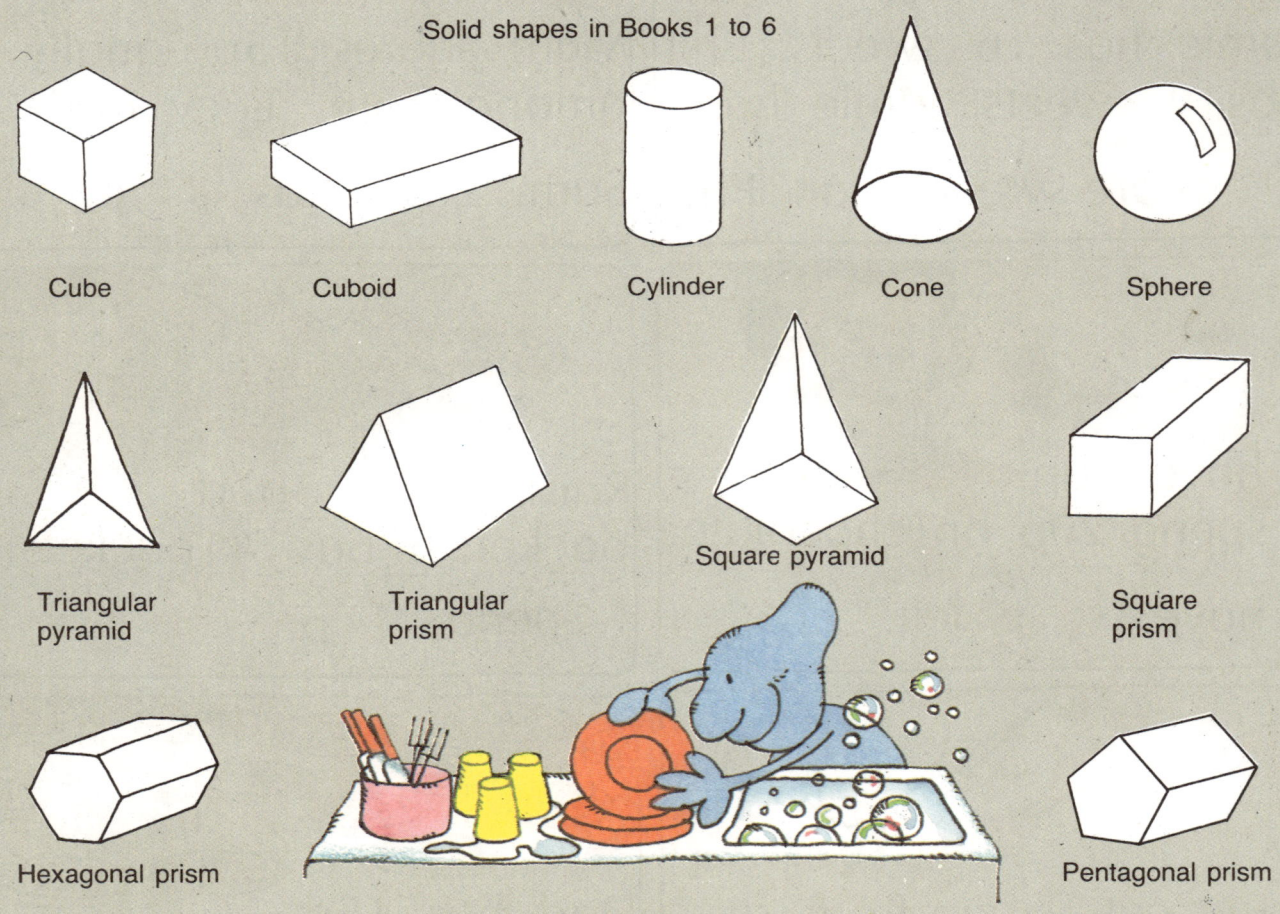

Cube   Cuboid   Cylinder   Cone   Sphere

Triangular pyramid   Triangular prism   Square pyramid   Square prism

Hexagonal prism   Pentagonal prism

Oliver & Boyd, Longman House, Burnt Mill,
Harlow, Essex, CM20 2JE

First published 1989

Produced by Longman Group FE Ltd. Printed in Hong Kong

Oliver & Boyd

ISBN 0-05-004381-1

9 780050 043813